Birthday Traditions around the World

Published by The Child's World®
1980 Lookout Drive • Mankato, MN 56003-1705
800-599-READ • www.childsworld.com

Acknowledgments
The Child's World®: Mary Berendes, Publishing Director
Red Line Editorial: Editorial direction
The Design Lab: Design
Amnet: Production

Design elements: Telnov Oleksii/Shutterstock Images

Photographs ©: Shutterstock Images, Cover, Title, 5, 29;
Nestor Noci/Shutterstock Images, 7; Morgan Lane Photography/
Shutterstock Images, 9; Kai Wong/Shutterstock Images, 12;
Phil McDonald/Shutterstock Images, 13; Eric Delmar/iStockphoto, 17;
Sadequl Hussain/Shutterstock Images, 20; iStockphoto, 21; AISPIX by
Image Source/Shutterstock Images, 25

ISBN 9781614734246
LCCN 2012946509

Printed in the United States of America
Mankato, MN
November, 2012
PA02145

Dedication
For Martha Rolf, who celebrates life so beautifully

About the Author

Ann Ingalls' first book, *The Little Piano Girl*, was published by Houghton Mifflin in January 2010. Pilgrim Press released her second book, *Worm Watching and Other Wonderful Ways to Teach Young Children to Pray*, in May 2012. Her first emergent reader, *Ice Cream Soup*, will hit shelves in June 2013. Visit Ann at www.anningallswrites.com.

About the Illustrator

Elisa Chavarri is a Peruvian illustrator who works from her home in Alpena, Michigan, which she shares with her husband, Matt, and her cat, Sergeant Tibbs. She has previously illustrated *Fly Blanky Fly*, by Anne Margaret Lewis, and *Fairly Fairy Tales*, by Esmé Raji Codell.

Table of Contents

Chapter One

Happy Birthday!

Birthdays are celebrated all over the world. Each country does this in its own way. But there are some similar things, too. Often families and friends come together. A favorite custom in many places is to place candles on the birthday cake—one for each year being celebrated.

The birthday person makes a wish and blows out the candles. Some people think if the birthday child blows all the candles out in one try, his or her wish will come true.

Make a wish!

Chapter Two

Birthdays in the Past

The **pharaohs** in ancient Egypt had big birthday parties. They held feasts, and everyone gave them gifts. But most ancient Egyptians did not **celebrate** birthdays.

Men in ancient Rome celebrated birthdays. They prayed and feasted on their birthdays. Roman leaders had big public parties. They held parades, put on plays, and ate lots of food.

The first birthday parties for children were in Germany around 1200 AD. The parties were called *Kinderfeste* (KIN-duh-fest-eh). Parents woke up their birthday child with a cake with birthday candles. The candles were kept lit until after dinner. Then the child made a secret wish and blew them out.

Chapter Three

Birthdays in the United States

Americans love birthday parties. They celebrate their own birthdays. They celebrate birthdays for famous people, including Martin Luther King Jr., Abraham Lincoln, and George Washington. They celebrate the country's birthday on the Fourth of July, too!

Balloons and streamers are hung at children's parties. Friends are invited to the party. Friends and family members often bring presents. Some birthday parties are huge. Dozens of people come. There might be clowns, a pony to ride, or even a petting zoo! Others are small. A birthday party might include just a few friends for a sleepover. All birthday parties are fun!

Many Americans celebrate birthdays with a cake. They top the cake with lit candles. Usually there is one candle for each year. People sing "Happy Birthday." Two sisters from Kentucky wrote the song in 1893. It has been **translated** into several languages.

Chapter Four

Birthdays in India

Many people in India follow Hinduism. The religion is based on Indian tradition and on being good. Hindi parents put honey in a new baby's mouth. They whisper God's name in his or her ear.

Indians celebrate birthdays with parties. Many people come and they have many good things to eat. They bring small presents for the birthday child. They say "*Janam Din ki badhai!*" (JA-nam DEEN KEE BAD-hai) This means "Happy Birthday" in Hindi. Hindi is one of India's many languages.

Most children in India wear uniforms to school. Birthday children can wear any clothes they want. Usually they get new clothes for their birthdays. At school, the birthday child gives chocolate to the other children.

Birthdays in Australia

At birthday parties in Australia, families serve small bites of food. They eat with their fingers. Australians love lamingtons. These are small squares of cake dipped in chocolate and coconut. Another favorite treat is fairy bread. This is buttered bread dipped into sugar sprinkles. Then it is cut into small triangles and enjoyed.

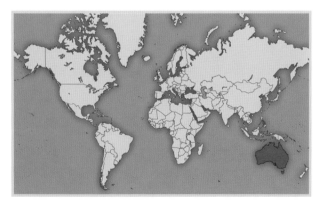

Chapter Six

Birthdays in Chile

People in Chile celebrate birthdays with a piñata. An animal is made of **papier-mâché**. The animal is filled with candy and small toys and is hung from a pole or a tree. Children hit the piñata with a stick to break it open. Their eyes are covered to make the game harder. Soon all the treats fall out!

People all over Central and South America break piñatas on their birthdays.

Chapter Seven

Birthdays in Ghana

Birthday children in Ghana eat *oto* (OH-toe) for breakfast. Oto is sweet potatoes mixed with onions. It is shaped into patties and fried. People eat hard-boiled eggs with the oto.

Later in the day, they have a party. They play a game known as *ampe* (AHM-puh). Ten to 12 children play. One player is the leader. The others stand in a semicircle. The leader faces the first player in the semicircle.

The leader and the player both clap hands. They jump in place at the same time. They each put one foot forward.

The leader is out if the two players put the same foot forward. The player then takes the leader's place. The leader scores a point if they put different feet forward. Then the leader plays with the next player.

Every player takes a turn as the leader. The one who scores the most points wins.

Chapter Eight

Birthdays in Israel

In Israel the birthday child wears a crown made from leaves or flowers. He or she sits in a chair **decorated** with streamers. Parents raise and lower the chair with the child in it one time for each year of age. They add one more lift for good luck. Guests sing and dance around the chair. The guests run races as they balance potatoes on spoons.

Many children in Israel are Jewish. The 13th birthday is special for a Jewish boy. On that day, he celebrates his Bar Mitzvah. A girl celebrates her Bat Mitzvah when she turns 12. Children are expected to obey Jewish laws after these ages. They are supposed to act like adults.

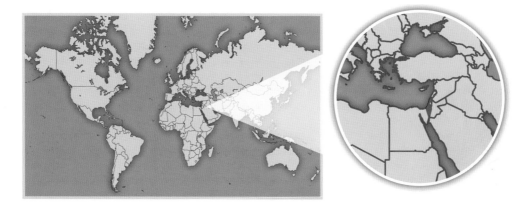

Chapter Nine

Birthdays in China

In China, the biggest celebrations are for newborns and the very old. Chinese people have great respect for their elders. They celebrate bringing a newborn into the family, too.

The parents of a new baby give red eggs to friends and family. They give even numbers of eggs for good luck. The color red means happiness in Chinese culture.

Relatives and friends of the family will give the child useful presents. The baby might get food or silverware. Most get money wrapped in red paper.

Adults eat **longevity** noodles on their birthdays. These noodles are very long. People try to eat the noodles without breaking them. This means they will have a long life!

Chapter Ten

Birthdays in Greece

Many people think the Greeks made the first birthday cake. They wanted to honor the goddess Artemis. One of her **symbols** is the moon. Ancient Greeks put candles on a cake to make it glow like the moon. They hoped the smoke from the candles would carry birthday wishes up to heaven.

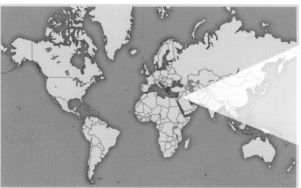

Chapter Eleven

Birthdays in Brazil

In Brazil, families decorate their houses with banners and colored paper flowers. Or they have birthday parties at special party halls. Sometimes they invite hundreds of guests. They set out a big table full of candy. Their favorite candy is *brigadeiros* (bri-gah-DAY-rohs). These are round chocolate candies.

Chapter Twelve

Birthdays in Korea

Koreans hold a feast 100 days after a baby's birth. They celebrate the baby's health and life. If the baby has been sick, the family has no party. It would be bad luck for the baby. Koreans honor the *samshin halmoni* (SAM-shin hal-MON-nee), or grandmother spirit. They give her offerings of rice and seaweed soup. They thank her for caring for the infant and mother.

Family and friends celebrate with rice cakes and wine. They take the rice cakes from dishes. They replace the rice cakes with bundles of thread. They wish for a long life for the child. Koreans also eat red and black bean cakes sweetened with sugar or honey.

Chapter Thirteen

Birthdays in Mexico

A Mexican girl's 15th birthday is a very special day. It is called *quinceañera* (keen-see-ah-NYAIR-ah). It is the day she becomes a grown-up.

Her family has a huge party. They save money for years to pay for it. The family goes to a special church service. The birthday girl wears a beautiful, fancy dress.

Then everyone goes to the party. There is dancing and music. There is food and a huge cake. The cake is dyed to match the birthday girl's dress!

Chapter Fourteen

Birthdays in Egypt

People in Egypt invite so many people to their parties that they have two birthday cakes. Only one cake has candles. They decorate their homes with paper garlands called *zeena* (ZEE-nah). These look like chains of snowflakes.

People in Egypt celebrate when a baby is one week old. This is called the *Sebou* (sih-BOO-uh). Friends and family come to see the newborn. They carry lighted candles and bring flowers and fruits. These are symbols of life and growth. They celebrate again when the baby turns one year old. Then there is lots of singing and dancing.

Birthday Song in Other Languages

ing these songs to the tune of "Happy Birthday"!

In Korean

Sang-il Chookha-Hapneeda
Sang-il Chookha-Hapneeda
Jul Guh Woon Sang-il Ulh
Chookha-Hapneeda

In Hebrew (Israel)

Yom Holedet Sameach
Yom Holedet Sameach
Yom Holedet Sameach
Yom Holedet Sameach

In French

Bonne Fete A Toi
Bonne Fete A Toi
Bonne Fete A *(birthday child's name)*
Bonne Fete A Toi

In German

Zum Geburtstag viel Glueck
Zum Geburtstag viel Glueck
Zum Geburtstag, lieber *(birthday child's name)*
Zum Geburstag viel Glueck

Make a Piñata

People in many countries celebrate their birthdays by breaking a piñata. Make a piñata for your next party!

Materials

Water
White glue
Newspaper ripped into long strips
Large balloon, blown up and tied shut
Paint or colored paper such as crepe paper or tissue paper, to decorate
String
Candy or small items to fill the piñata

Directions

1. Mix one part water with two parts white glue. Get an adult to help with this step.
2. Dip newspaper strips into the glue. Scrape off the extra glue. Stick the paper strips to the balloon until the whole balloon is covered. Leave a hole around the balloon tie so you can fill your piñata later. Let the first layer dry, then repeat two or three more times.
3. When the piñata is dry, pop the balloon and pull it out. Then decorate the piñata. Paint it or use glue without water to glue on colored paper.
4. Ask an adult to help you punch four small holes around the large hole. Thread string through the holes to hang the piñata. Fill the piñata with candy or other small items, and start the party!

Glossary

celebrated (SEL-uh-bray-ted) If something is celebrated, it is observed or taken notice of. People have celebrated birthdays for many years.

decorated (DEK-uh-rat-id) Something decorated has been made pretty. We decorated our house for the birthday party.

longevity (lawn-JEH-vih-tee) Longevity is having a long life. People wish for longevity on their birthdays.

papier-mâché (pay-per-mah-SHAY) Papier-mâché is paper that dries hard after it has been soaked in glue. Piñatas are made from papier-mâché.

pharaohs (FAIR-oh) Pharaohs were the kings of ancient Egypt. The pharaohs celebrated their birthdays.

symbols (SIM-buhls) Symbols are objects or signs that stand for something else. Hearts and the color red are symbols for love.

translated (trans-LATE-id) Something translated has been changed from one language into another. People have translated "Happy Birthday" into many languages.

Learn More

Books

Lankford, Mary D. *Birthdays around the World*. New York: Harper Collins, 2002.

Wallace, Paula S. *The World of Birthdays*. Milwaukee, WI: Gareth Stevens, 2003.

Web Sites

Visit our Web site for links about birthday traditions around the world: ***childsworld.com/links***

Note to Parents, Teachers, and Librarians: We routinely verify our Web links to make sure they are safe and active sites. So encourage your readers to check them out!

Index